HUNGARY
A PICTURE MEMORY

CLB 2577
© 1990 Colour Library Books Ltd, Godalming, Surrey, England.
All rights reserved.
Color separations by Scantrans Pte Ltd, Singapore.
This 1990 edition published by Crescent Books,
distributed by Outlet Book Company, Inc, a Random House Company,
225 Park Avenue South, New York, New York 10003.
Printed and bound in Italy.
ISBN 0 517 03384 4
8 7 6 5 4 3 2 1

Text
Tim Sharman

Design
Teddy Hartshorn

Photography
FPG International
International Stock Photo
Tim Sharman
Woodfin Camp and Associates, Inc

Picture Editor
Annette Lerner

Commissioning Editor
Andrew Preston

Publishing Assistant
Edward Doling

Editorial
Fleur Robertson
Gill Waugh

Production
Ruth Arthur
Sally Connolly
David Proffit

Director of Production
Gerald Hughes

Director of Publishing
David Gibbon

HUNGARY
A PICTURE MEMORY

CRESCENT BOOKS
NEW YORK

Close to the bright lights and smart shops of modern Budapest, in a darkened upper floor gallery protected by armed guards, lies one of the great artistic treasures of European history. Alone on a velvet cushion, eerily illuminated by spotlights, sits a glittering crown adorned with filigree gold and richly colored, exquisitely crafted enamel figures, obviously Byzantine in style. Dating from the eleventh century, the story of this exotic headpiece, with its famous bent cross that no one dares to straighten, very much reflects the history of the Hungarian nation.

Of obscure origin, sometimes lost, stolen or held to ransom, the crown spent the years after the Second World War locked away in the USA, a hostage to history. In 1978, with the Hungarians acknowledged to be the acceptable face of world communism, the crown was restored to its rightful owners with due pomp and ceremony, and ever since it has been the focal point of every school outing to the capital.

If the origin of the crown is obscure and much debated, so is that of the Hungarian people themselves. In order to understand the people who have survived years of Communist rule in better shape than most countries of Eastern Europe, it is necessary to return to those centuries following the fall of the Roman Empire north of the Alps. The Romans crumpled under the repeated onslaughts of those tribes who were part of the great and still mysterious migration westward from the Asian steppes in the first centuries AD. In the fifth century one of the most infamous tribal leaders, Attila, king of the Huns, made his base in the fertile plains of the middle Danube and gave the region the name by which it is still known to most of the world. It was not until the ninth century, however, that the present occupiers of Hungary, the Magyars, crossed the Carpathian Mountains and discovered the lovely lands of Transylvania and the basin of the Danube. Initially this was not enough for them, and these strong and aggressive warriors stampeded around the more civilized lands to the west, reaching Spain and the Atlantic coast and wreaking havoc as they went.

It did not take the Christian rulers of the region long to unite and inflict several defeats upon the Magyars who, realising that Europe was too crowded and disciplined for their hooligan tactics, settled down to a pastoral life. And so it was that in 1000 AD, in a church on a hill overlooking the Danube, the most famous of the Magyar leaders, Stephen (later St. Stephen), was crowned under the watchful eye of the German Emperor and several of his nobles. Fragments of that original church at Esztergom have been found beneath a later cathedral, which to this day remains the seat of the Hungarian primate. For forty years Stephen ruled his kingdom, and a strong Magyar nation state, faithful to the Church of Rome, quickly developed. Visiting the country in 1116, the Dean of Prague wrote, "The Magyar people is mighty and powerful, very wealthy and irresistible in weapons of war, capable of fighting any monarch in the wide world'. But neither a nation nor its leaders can stay strong for ever, and the millenium since Stephen has seen the power and wealth of Hungary rise and fall spectacularly. Such a tumultuous history meant much building of castles, palaces and fortified towns, many of which have survived to provide a catalogue of architectural styles that ranges from the medieval to the recent and often splendid buildings produced by the present generation.

In fact, Hungary's heritage goes back much farther because, for the first four hundred years of the Christian era, the lands up to the Danube were firmly held as the Roman province of Pannoia, and liberally scattered through western Hungary, from Budapest to the Austrian frontier, are remains of that greatest of all European empires. In the capital, two complete Roman towns, one military, one civil, have been unearthed, and today slender marble columns stand amid modern shopping centers and an amphitheater serves as a traffic roundabout. Elsewhere, there are wonderful mosaics, villas, aqueducts and milestones – even a stretch of original paved road, which is a testament to the prowess of those Roman engineers.

The great period of Hungarian castle-building began after the retreat of the Mongol hordes, which had swept through Europe in 1241 as the Magyars had a few centuries before. Firmly established as a regional power by then, the Magyars had much to lose, so within a few years most towns were protected by strong fortifications, and these can still be seen in many places. Two great figures dominated the monarchy in this period. The long reign of Béla IV in the thirteenth century restored the nation after the Mongol raids and consolidated the power structure, and, after Louis the Great's forty-year rule, Hungary entered the fifteenth century with a territory stretching from the Carpathian watershed in the north and east right down to the Adriatic coast of Dalmatia.

For the uninitiated traveller, the biggest surprise in Hungary is coming across minarets more often found in the Islamic Middle East. Fine examples can be seen in Eger in the north and in Pécs in the south, close to the border with Yugoslavia. Together with the Turkish baths still operating in Budapest, they are a reminder of the dark days of the sixteenth and seventeenth centuries when much of southeastern Europe fell to the Turks. The Hungarians fought many campaigns against them, the military commander János Hunyadi becoming a great national hero in the process, but in 1526, the most infamous date in their history, the Hungarian army was defeated and their young king killed at Mohács, beside the Danube to the south of Budapest. For more than 150 years most Hungarian lands were settled by the Turks, who turned many of the existing churches into mosques and devastated great areas of the country.

Finally, after being driven out by an international army of the West following the 1683 siege of Vienna, the Turks retreated to the Balkans, and it was the turn of the powerful Habsburg dynasty, based in Vienna, to lay claim to the Magyar lands. The eighteenth and nineteenth centuries were dominated by the struggle between Vienna and the various Hungarian claimants to the throne – during this time the development of the country came a poor second to political intrigue and sometimes outright war. As the cult of nationalism spread through Europe it was once again a time for martyrs and heroes, and the names now seen on streets and squares throughout the country recall those times. Among the most famous are Ferenc Rákóczi, a noble who put his reputation and fortune to the service and struggle against Vienna, and Lajos Kossuth, who took advantage of the turmoil of that year of revolutions, 1848, to declare Hungary independent. He even toured America to raise support for the cause, becoming very popular in the process, but once again the superior force of the Habsburgs, with more than a little help from the Russian Tsar, won the day.

Finally, in 1867, the famous "Compromise" was agreed and Hungary was elevated to the position of joint leader of the Habsburg lands, which were re-christened the Austro-Hungarian Empire, and the young emperor Franz-Josef was crowned King of Hungary in a spectacular ceremony in Budapest. From that time onwards, Budapest blossomed, developing from an elegant provincial capital into a large, modern city that could boast Parisian-style boulevards and a marvellous riverside Parliament building which rivals Westminster. In 1896 the nation celebrated a thousand years on European soil and the city was gave a great party. The first electric subway line on mainland Europe carried the populace out to a large public park with its own museums, monuments and thermal baths, while in the city center Art Nouveau offices and shops enlivened the streets. Yet all too soon the party was over.

The First World War shook the complex jigsaw puzzle of Europe to its very foundations and afterwards, when the pieces came to rest, the map had a very different look about it. Gone was the Austro-Hungarian Empire, and in its place emerged the brand new countries of Czechoslovakia and Yugoslavia, whilst Hungary, once so mighty, was reduced to its present small size. The northern hill country of Slovakia had gone, as had the rich lands of Transylvania, which were given to a much enlarged Romania, while the country's route to the Adriatic ports was now blocked by Slavic Yugoslavia. There was much bitterness amongst Hungarians directed against the Trianon Treaty which had decided these matters.

The years between the wars started confusingly. A year as a liberal social-democratic republic was followed by just 133 days of local Communist rule. Stability, if not joy, came with the arrival – legend has it on a white horse – of Admiral Miklós Horthy, a Hungarian squire who spent his career in the service of the old Emperor. Calling himself Regent and never actually abolishing the now vacant monarchy, he ruled the country until forced into a reluctant association with Hitler, which at least kept the Nazi occupation and all its terrors at bay until 1944.

Then came Budapest's darkest hour. Without doubt, Buda and Pest, located on either side of the Danube river, are the among the most beautiful cities in Europe, yet, regardless of this fact, the Nazis blew up all the bridges and turned the ancient castle district of Buda on the high west bank of the Danube into a fortress to face the rapidly advancing Soviet army. In the ensuing weeks of bitter fighting the palace and the city's network of lovely baroque streets and old churches became little more than rubble. By the end of the war, it was clear that in the small space of some twenty-five years Hungary had been reduced from a great kingdom to a small and broken land with an imposed Communist government led by some very unsavory characters. In 1956, after the country's famous popular uprising against Communist domination, Soviet tanks came back again – this time to kill Hungarians.

When visiting Budapest today all this violence seems of another era. The city is once again the business center and playground of the region, the castle district has been rebuilt and now shines in the waters of the Danube, and the comfortable old Habsburg cafés are full of coffee drinkers and cake eaters deep in debate or gossip. The narrow canyon of Váci Street on the flat Pest side of the river shimmers with high-fashion boutiques, but still finds room for several literary bookshops. Voracious readers, the Hungarians are an energetic and educated people, aware of the complexities of the world and anxious to make their mark on it. Some already have. Dr Ernest Rubik and his famous cube, for example, can be seen to represent the modern Hungary – a country with few resources other than the ingenuity and intelligence of its people.

There is, however, one natural resource which is put to good use and that is the thermal water which bubbles to the surface in hundreds of springs throughout the country and has been famed since Roman times. Of great therapeutic value for a variety of aches and pains, these springs now attract patients from many countries to the modern hotels built beside them.

Without doubt, Hungary today is a land of great contrasts. Outside the humming city, indeed visible from the capital's Castle Hill, lies the Great Hungarian Plain, famous for its empty horizon, its cattle and its cowboys. Once the bed of an inland sea, this *puszta* is now less a grassy wilderness than a gigantic farm where wheat flourishes and a billion sunflowers follow the bright summer light. But deep in its interior, far away from the few main roads which cross it, there are little dusty villages of pastel colored cottages where chicken scratch, cats doze and the notes of a cymbalom can be heard from the café.

The old ways are not forgotten here, the songs and customs of the shepherds are easily recalled. Much of the land is pure sand and many roads are unpaved. On the Hortobágy *puszta*, once home to millions of cattle which were traded throughout Europe, displays of horsemanship and folk art are provided for the tourists. But not everywhere is as flat and moody as the plain. West of the Danube the landscape is mostly one of gently undulating hills, beyond which the larger foothills of the eastern Alps loom across the Austrian border.

Across the northeast of the country there is a substantial range of forested hills which extend west of the Danube to provide a backdrop for Hungary's great Lake Balaton. This narrow, fifty-mile-long stretch of shallow water, whose northern shore is smothered in vines and summer houses, is a traditional holiday center not only for Hungarians, but also for families from Germany, Czechoslovakia and Poland. Sailing and fishing are the great pastimes here now, the lake remaining as popular today as when the Romans came here to retire or recuperate. On the wooded Tihany peninsula, the loveliest spot on the lake and now a national park, the baroque towers of the abbey church stand over a crypt built in 1055 to house the tomb of King András I, who died five years later.

Even before political changes re-shaped Eastern Europe, Hungary had a relaxed and confident society, which for twenty years has been moving towards a market economy. Budapest's finest restaurants and many of its shops have long been in private hands, local businesses operate around the world and many joint ventures with Austrian companies, for example, have been operating for years. As with other former socialist countries, the young generation is on the whole well-educated and worldly. Since Magyar bears no relationship to any major language, Hungarians have been quick to learn others in order to speak to the world.

During the nineteenth century Hungary's artists and musicians traveled the world and achieved great fame. Franz Liszt was a superstar pianist in the mid-nineteenth century, and the painter Mihaly Munkacsy – almost unknown in the West today – toured America in the 1880s selling his pictures for huge sums of money. A century earlier, Josef Haydn had been in residence at the great Esterhazy palace in western Hungary, and recitals of his music are still a highlight of the cultural year. All over Hungary, chamber concerts are held in castle courtyards and ballrooms, film festivals in the cities, there are several opera and dance companies in the country and old folk ceremonies are still performed in the villages.

In such towns as Pécs, with its almost Mediterranean climate, Eger against the northern hills, Koszeg and Sopron in the far west and Veszprém close to Lake Balaton, as well as in Budapest, Hungary has a collection of fine and fascinating old towns, full of character and charm and boasting many historically important buildings. The toy-town roof tops of Sopron, the thirteenth-century Romanesque church with its extraordinary carved doorway in the village of Ják, the tiny wooden churches close to the Romanian border and the great castle Eger – all are important cultural and artistic treasures not only of Hungary but of the whole continent. Fortunately, they have been cared for and restored by an army of devoted archaeologists and craftsmen.

For many centuries merchants have travelled to the warm, dry hills overlooking the Great Plain to buy the fine wines of Tokaj and Eger, making them famous throughout Europe. Today this is still big business; good wines are produced throughout the country and many of them have gained an international reputation. In more recent years the light soils of the Plain have been used to grow enormous quantities of fruit, including apricots, peaches, apples and cherries, most of which is exported. Manufacturing industry did not develop until the later years of the last century, but the skill of the Hungarian engineers has been recognized; the largest plant in Budapest, which makes railway carriages and locomotives, was one of the very first European companies to be taken over by a Western company.

With their political institutions having made the difficult transition to democracy without unrest, and their glorious Parliament building once again a serious debating chamber, Hungarians can approach the new century with confidence. Fully aware of the problems of surviving in the "cut and thrust" of the open market today, they have a rich culture and heritage intact to sustain them and their future looks bright.

Facing page: the Hungarian Parliament Building.

These pages: Budapest, Hungary's capital. The
rocky hill of Buda on the west bank of the Danube
was first settled in prehistoric times and became
the site of a Hungarian royal castle in the thirteenth
century. Buda's, and Hungary's, golden age was in
the fifteenth century under the enlightened King
Mátyás, whose Renaissance court attracted artists
from all over Europe. Time and war have eroded
most of the medieval city, and even the glorious
Mátyás church with its colored roof and neo-gothic
spire is the result of inspired nineteenth-century
rebuilding. Overleaf: a view north across Budapest
and the River Danube.

The British-built Chain Bridge (below), opened in 1848, was the first permanent link between Buda and Pest. In 1873 the two towns were united as Budapest, and there followed a period of rapid growth which saw the building of the Parliament (above left and facing page), the recreation of the Mátyás Church (above) and the extension to its vast size of the baroque Royal Palace (below left). In 1896 Hungarians celebrated a thousand years of settlement in the Danube basin by creating a spacious Heroes Square, dominated by the Millenium Monument (left).

Today some two million of Hungary's ten million people live in Budapest, which, in the new post-Communist era, is vying to become the capital of central Europe. Pest's busy boulevards (facing page and right) are a stark contrast to the narrow streets and relative peace of Buda's Castle Hill, where the Arany Hordó – Golden Barrel – Beer House (above right) dates from the fourteenth century. The little houses in Fortuna Street (below right) date from the seventeenth century. Above: a Budapest mailbox. Below: folk musicians entertain visitors to Castle Hill (overleaf).

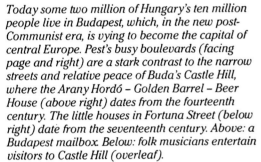

The natural fortress of Buda's Castle Hill, with its medieval Old Town (above and facing page) has not proved impregnable. It was occupied by the Ottoman Turks from 1541 until 1686, when they were finally overthrown, much damage being done to the architecture in the process. Sadly much of the city was devastated again in 1945 as the German army fought vainly against defeat. Amongst the landmarks which have since been restored is the Fisherman's Bastion (right and below right), built at the turn of the century and, across the river in Pest, the Parisian shopping arcade (below), of the same period.

The Hungarian countryside is both beautiful and busy. Above Budapest the River Danube (previous pages) cuts through the northern hills where the famous white Lippizaners (below), the famous dressage and carriage horses, are bred.

Hungarians delight in their countryside. Summer houses with their tiny vineyards dot many slopes (facing page top) and everywhere there are fishermen (facing page bottom). Overleaf: the great northern forests, much favored by walkers.

Many ancient towns and villages lie along the edge of Hungary's northern hills, often sited where trade routes crossed from the old kingdom of Poland. Most historic is Eger (above left and overleaf), famous for its Bull's Blood wine and its heroic defense against the Turks in 1552. The minaret built by the Turks still stands. Hungary's second largest city is the steel town of Miskolc (above and left). Sarospatak (below left) is a quiet town close to the Soviet frontier, while Gyöngyös (below) has the best telephone boxes. Tiny Hollokõ (facing page) is isolated and unspoiled.

To the east of Budapest the Great Hungarian Plain (these pages) stretches as flat as a table to the mountains of Transylvania. The plain is the nation's wheat bowl, a prairie dominated by large state and co-operative farms. Seemingly featureless, it supports countless little villages and isolated farmsteads (below) in its vastness. Many roads have no surface other than the dust of this dry region, and for villagers the bicyle (left) is the standard mode of transport. Older cottages are made with mud-and-straw bricks and thatched with reeds (below left). Farmworkers have long been allowed to work small private plots (bottom left) for profit.

Many Hungarians are still employed on the land, but more and more young people move to the cities for education and work, leaving an ageing population in the countryside who cling to old habits and customs. Paprika (above left) is vital to much of Hungarian cuisine and is used in those most famous local products, goulash and salami. Chamomile (left and below) for tea and hops (below left) are also widely grown, while the packed lunch (facing page) and the bicycle (above) are seen everywhere on the plain.

The horse has played a major role in the history of the Magyar people, carrying them in the tenth century from their earlier homeland on the Asian steppes. The breeding of cattle (left) in the region also dates from those nomadic days and is still an important business. Below left: a horseman shows off his skills in Bugac Puszta in Kiskunsag National Park. Facing page top: "Csikós" cowboys. As well as the Danube, several other rivers dissect the plain, providing good fishing (below and facing page bottom), as well as reeds (above) for thatching.

Szeged, on the River Tisza, is the largest and most important economic and cultural center south of the Great Plain, the private market (these pages) attracting both buyers and sellers from the surrounding countryside. Today it is a frontier town with Romania and Yugoslavia, but before the 1918 frontier changes, which drastically reduced the size of Hungary, it served a large area of the Banat to the south and Transylvania to the east. Situated on the main route to Greece and Turkey, it is a major transport center and also produces large amounts of paprika and spicy salami.

Pécs (these pages), close to the Yugoslav border in the south, was the chief town of the Roman province of Pannonia and is one of the oldest settlements in Hungary, in the third century becoming the chief town of the Roman province of Pannonia. The foundations of the Romanesque cathedral (above) date from the eleventh century, and in 1367 the town was the setting of the first Hungarian university. The large, nineteenth-century town hall (facing page) dominates the main square, while the synagogue (above right) is a reminder of the large Jewish population in pre-Hitler days. The roof tiles of the new department store (below) were manufactured locally.

Pécs (these pages) occupies the southern slopes of the Mecsek Mountains, the modern industrial area of the city spreading onto the plain below.

The warm hillsides (facing page) of Pécs produce the sparkling Pannonia champagne of the region.

Facing page: gently undulating landscapes dotted with baroque churches in western Hungary.

The Danube (below) separates the Great Plain from Transdanubian lands to the west.

Lake Balaton (these pages), in the heart of Transdanubia, is the playground of Hungary and, as such, the holiday center for millions of Central Europeans. This extraordinary stretch of water, forty-eight miles long but never more than a few miles wide, is a warm and shallow survivor of the inland sea which covered the middle-Danube basin in prehistoric times. The Romans built villas here, as do prosperous Hungarians today, the 120-mile shoreline being an almost continuous thread of villages, resorts and campsites. The hilly north shore (below) produces most of Hungary's wine, but has also polluted the lake with chemical run-off, now subject to tight controls.

The Benedictine Abbey of Tihany (below) stands high above Lake Balaton on a wooded peninsula, and at the western end of the lake is the Festetics Palace (above right) built in 1745. In 1797 Count György Festetics founded Europe's finest agricultural institute, now a university here. Above: thatching reeds cut from the water's edge. A few miles west is the famous thermal spring of Hévíz (below right), one of many medicinal spas in Hungary, and further west, near the Austrian border, lie the towns of Szombathely (facing page) and Kőszeg (right). Overleaf: a typical western Hungary landscape.

Székesfehérvár (above), Hungary's oldest town, was the capital of the nation's founding father, Stephen I. Many of Hungary's most interesting old towns lie in the hills to the north of Lake Balaton, the largest being Veszprém (above left and below), dominated by its Bishop's Palace and cathedral. Tapolca (left) lies close to modern bauxite quarries, while Nagyvázsony (below left and overleaf) is today a quiet village famed for its riding center, although in the wars against the Turks its castle (facing page) saw much action. Following page: a quiet backwater of the Danube.